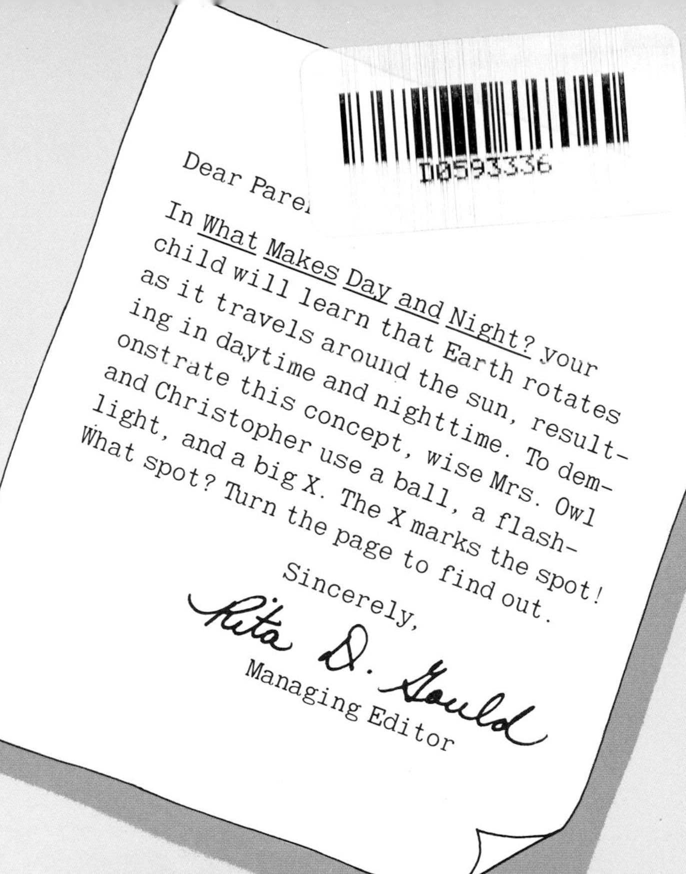

Dear Pare

In *What Makes Day and Night?* your child will learn that Earth rotates as it travels around the sun, resulting in daytime and nighttime. To demonstrate this concept, wise Mrs. Owl and Christopher use a ball, a flashlight, and a big X. The X marks the spot! What spot? Turn the page to find out.

Sincerely,

Rita D. Gould

Managing Editor

FAMILY FUN

- Reenact with your child Mrs. Owl's demonstration of Earth's rotation and orbit. First, on the ground outline a path representing Earth's orbit. Next, role-playing the sun, your child can shine a flashlight on you (role-playing Earth) as you rotate and orbit the sun. Then reverse positions and try the reenactment again.
- Using a large sheet of paper, help your child draw pictures of activities he or she does when it is day and activities he or she does when it is night.

READ MORE ABOUT IT

- *What Are Seasons?*
- *What Is the Moon?*

This book is a presentation of Weekly Reader Books.
Weekly Reader Books Offers book clubs for children
from preschool through high school.
For further information write to: Newfield Publications, Inc.,
4343 Equity Drive, Columbus, Ohio 43228

This edition is published by arrangement
with Checkerboard Press, Inc.

Printed in the United States of America
by Checkerboard Press.

WEEKLY READER BOOKS presents

What Makes Day and Night?

A **Just Ask**™ Book

Original title: Why Is It Dark?

by Chris Arvetis
and Carole Palmer

illustrated by
James Buckley

NEWFIELD PUBLICATIONS
MIDDLETOWN, CT.

We have to stop.
It's getting too dark
to play.

It is getting dark!
Every day it gets dark. I wonder why?

Each day the sun seems to disappear from the sky. Let's go see Mrs. Owl. Maybe she can tell us why !

Mrs. Owl
will know!
She is
smart!

Can you tell us, Mrs. Owl, why it gets dark?
I want to know too!

Why yes,
I think I can.

First of all, we live on the earth.
The earth is a PLANET.
Say it with me–PLAN–ET.
PLAN–ET!

PLAN–ET!
PLAN–ET!

The planet earth goes
around the sun.
The path the earth takes
is called its ORBIT.
Can you say that ?
OR–BIT !
OR–BIT !

Let me show you.
We'll use a ball
for the planet earth,
and we'll pretend the
flashlight is the sun.
Interesting!

Hmmm!

You take the earth.
Start here and walk
around the sun.
Make a big path.

Go all the way around. It takes the earth about 365 days to go around the sun. That's one year.
Follow the path!

365 days!
That is one year!

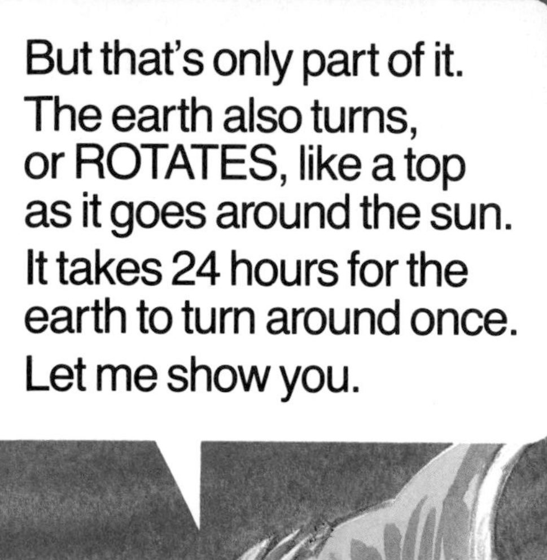
But that's only part of it.
The earth also turns,
or ROTATES, like a top
as it goes around the sun.
It takes 24 hours for the
earth to turn around once.
Let me show you.

The X marks where we live on the earth.
The flashlight is the sun shining on the earth.
When the sun is shining on that side of the earth where the X is, it is daytime.
It is light on this side!

As the earth turns, that part faces away from the sun. Then it is nighttime where we live– and it is dark!

It is dark
on this side!
Fascinating!

Or, to look at it another way, just imagine this... When it is daytime where Christopher lives, it is dark on the other side of the world, where another mouse will be fast asleep.

And 12 hours later it will be the other way around!
I get it!

Let's look at the sun
and the earth again.
This little ball is the moon.
Just as the earth orbits
the sun, the moon goes
around the earth.

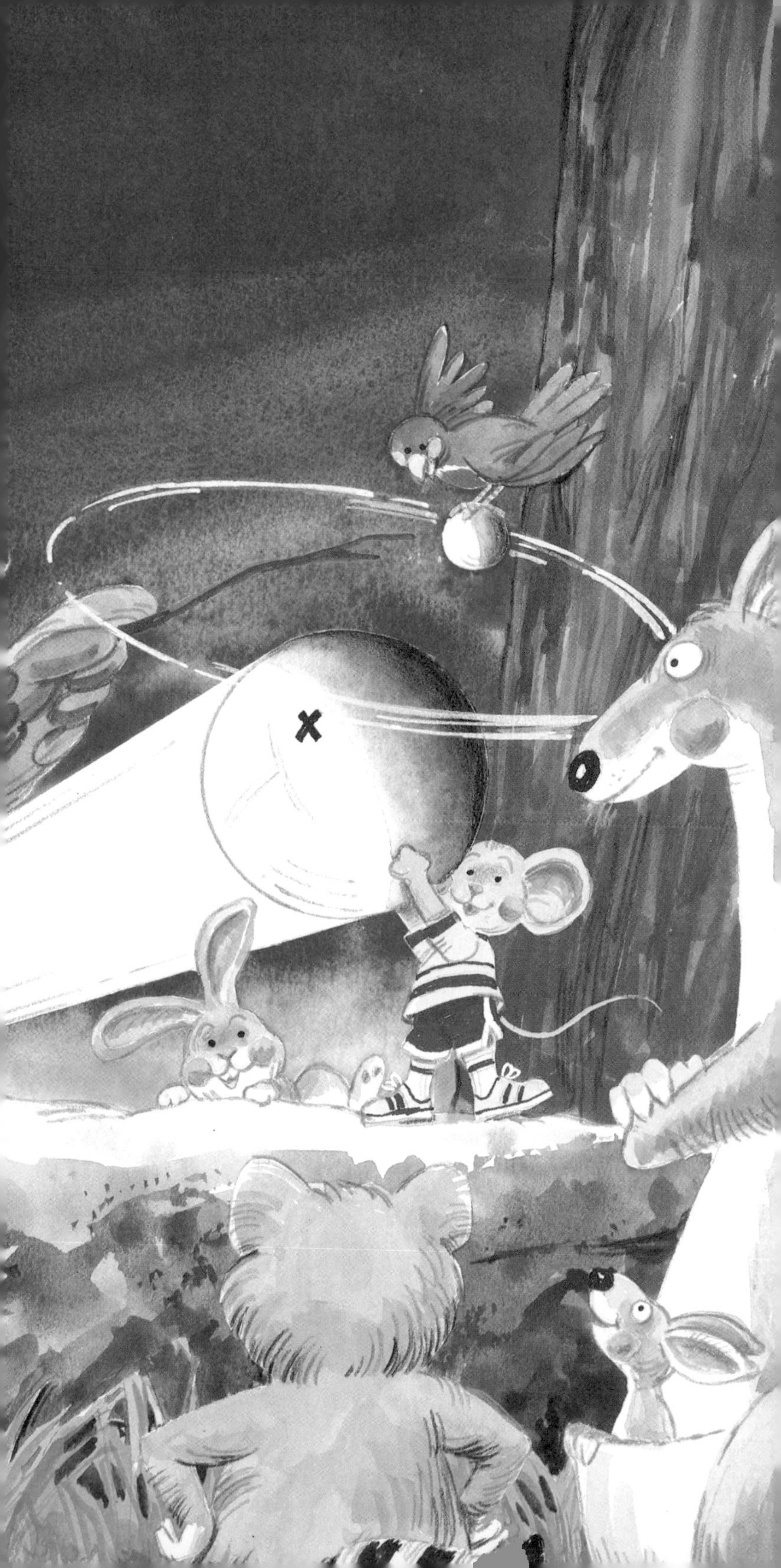

Look at my picture.
The sun's light shines on the earth and the moon.
Then the sunlight REFLECTS, or bounces off, the moon.

Did you know that?
Did you?

We see the bright moon in the sky, so it is a lot less dark even though it is night.

I knew that!

Just remember–
The earth goes around the sun.
When our part of the earth faces the sun, it is day.
When it faces away from the sun, it is night.
And it is dark.

The earth
is turning
all the time!
Wow!

Now I know
why it is dark!
We do too!
Me too!